"Parents Raising Money-Smart Kids: A Guide for Ideas and Conversations."

Empowering your kids with financial wisdom.

Creating opportunities to start that money conversation early.

Written by:

 Chat GPT

CASH CRUNCH GAMES

"Parents Raising Money-Smart Kids: A Guide for Ideas and Conversations."

Forward:

In today's rapidly changing world, the importance of financial literacy has never been greater. The ability to manage money wisely and make informed financial decisions is a critical life skill that can empower individuals and pave the way for a secure and prosperous future. While schools play a vital role in imparting academic knowledge, the responsibility of teaching financial skills often falls upon the shoulders of parents and grandparents.

"Parents Raising Money-Smart Kids: A Guide for Ideas and Conversations" is a comprehensive guide that recognizes the influential role that parents and grandparents play in shaping the financial habits and attitudes of the younger generation. This book serves as a compass, providing invaluable guidance and practical advice to help families navigate the complex world of personal finance.

Within these pages, you will find a treasure trove of insights, strategies, and activities designed to empower parents and grandparents with the tools they need to instill healthy financial habits into their children and grandchildren. From starting early and building a solid foundation to introducing concepts like budgeting, saving, and responsible spending, this book offers a roadmap for cultivating a strong financial mindset in the next generation.

What sets this book apart is its emphasis on the unique perspectives and experiences of parents and grandparents and the wealth of wisdom and life experiences, that bring a distinct value to the table allowing for stories to be shared and timeless lessons to be imparted, while serving as role models for financial prudence. This book highlights the invaluable role parents and grandparents can play in nurturing financial literacy, bridging the generational gap, and creating a legacy of financial well-being.

Through engaging anecdotes, practical tips, and actionable steps, this book encourages a collaborative approach to financial education. It emphasizes the importance of open communication, shared financial goals, and involving children in money discussions from an early age.

By working together, parents and grandparents can create a supportive environment that fosters financial literacy, resilience, and a sense of financial empowerment.

"Parents Raising Money-Smart Kids: A Guide for Ideas and Conversations" is not just a book; it is a call to action. It is a reminder that every conversation about money, every lesson in budgeting, and every decision to save can shape the financial future of our children and grandchildren. It is an invitation for parents and grandparents to join hands and become financial mentors, guiding the younger generation towards a lifetime of financial success.

I invite you to embark on this transformative journey, exploring the power you possess as parents and grandparents to make a lasting impact on the financial well-being of your loved ones.

Together, let us equip the next generation with the knowledge, skills, and confidence they need to navigate the ever-changing financial landscape and embrace a future of financial independence.

*****For the sake of repetition and simplicity*****

This book is for parents and grandparents to use with one child/grandchild or multiple children/grandchildren. For the sake of repetition and simplicity, the terms "parent" and "children" will be utilized throughout the book, however, those terms could be substituted with "grandparent" and "grandchildren". In some chapters there may well be some repetition. This is done in a way that looks at differing perspectives and development of points.

Contents:

Chapter 1.

Why Should We be Introducing Basic Financial Concepts at a Young Age?

Introducing basic financial concepts at a young age is crucial for several reasons:

1. **Building a Strong Foundation**: Just like any other skill, financial literacy is best developed from a young age. By introducing basic financial concepts early on, children can build a strong foundation and develop healthy financial habits that will benefit them throughout their lives.

2. **Forming Positive Money Mindsets**: Introducing financial concepts early helps shape children's attitudes and perceptions towards money. It enables them to understand the value of money, appreciate the importance of saving, and develop a responsible approach to spending.

3. **Developing Critical Thinking Skills**: Financial concepts involve decision-making, problem-solving, and critical thinking. Introducing these concepts at a young age encourages children to think critically about money-related choices, consider the consequences of their actions, and make informed financial decisions.

4. Promoting Financial Responsibility: Early exposure to financial concepts empowers children to take responsibility for their own money. It teaches them the importance of managing their finances, setting goals, and making choices that align with their financial priorities.

5. Instilling a Savings Habit: Introducing basic financial concepts includes teaching children the importance of saving. By instilling a savings habit early on, children learn to delay gratification, set goals, and accumulate funds for future needs and aspirations.

6. Fostering Independence: Financial literacy equips children with the knowledge and skills to become financially independent. Introducing basic financial concepts allows children to gain a sense of control over their own money, promoting independence and self-reliance.

7. Empowering Future Decision-Making: As children grow older, they will face more complex financial decisions. By introducing basic financial concepts at a young age, they develop a foundation that prepares them to navigate financial challenges and make informed choices in the future.

8. **Avoiding Costly Mistakes**: Lack of financial knowledge can lead to costly mistakes later in life. By introducing basic financial concepts early, children can learn about budgeting, managing debt, and avoiding financial pitfalls, helping them make smarter financial decisions as adults.

In summary, introducing basic financial concepts at a young age sets the stage for a lifetime of financial well-being. It empowers children with the knowledge, skills, and confidence that they need to make informed financial decisions, achieve their goals, and ultimately build a secure financial future.

Notes:

....

....

....

Money Fact: The original Monopoly board game included real money up until the 1940s.

Chapter 2.

How do Parents Explain the Value of Money to Their Children?

Explaining the value of money to a child is important to help them develop a healthy understanding of money and its significance. Here's an example of how a parent might explain the value of money:

Money is more than just pieces of paper or metal coins. It represents something very important in our lives: the things we need and want. Just like we exchange our time and effort for money when we work, we can use money to get things that make our lives better and more enjoyable.

Money has value because it allows us to provide for our basic needs like food, clothing, and shelter. It also gives us the opportunity to pursue our dreams and enjoy experiences that bring us happiness. When we use money wisely, it can help us create a secure and fulfilling life.

But it's also important to understand that money is not limitless. We only get so much over a certain period of time. If, for example, you get a weekly allowance, all you have is what you receive each week (unless you do extra chores or jobs). We have to make choices about how we use it because there are always more things that we want than the money we have. This means we need to think about what's most important to us and make decisions that align with our values and goals.

Sometimes, we have to save our money to buy something we really want in the future. Saving means being patient and putting aside a little bit of money each time we receive it. It's like collecting puzzle pieces to complete a picture. The more we save, the closer we get to our goal.

We should also be mindful of our spending and not waste money on things we don't truly need or that won't bring us long-term happiness. It's like making choices between buying a toy that might be fun for a short time or saving for a family outing or a special item that will bring us lasting joy.

Remember, the value of money goes beyond the things that we buy. It is about understanding the time taken and the hard work and effort it takes to earn money and in using it wisely to create a better life for ourselves and those we care about. By making smart choices with our money, we can achieve our dreams, help others, and find true fulfillment.

Notes:

....

....

....

Money Fact: The word "salary" is a Latin word "salarium" used in Roman times when Roman Soldiers were paid a handful of salt each day (which was worth more than gold in its day). Salt was essential for preserving their food.

Chapter 3.

How do Parents Explain Comparison Shopping to Their Children?

Explaining comparison shopping can help children develop smart consumer habits and make informed purchasing decisions. Here's an example of how you might explain comparison shopping:

Comparison shopping is like being a detective or a super-sleuth when it comes to buying things. It means taking the time to look at different options and comparing them to find the best choice. Just like when we're solving a puzzle or finding clues, comparison shopping helps us make smart decisions with our money.

When we want to buy something, it's important not to rush into it. We should explore different stores, websites, or brands that offer the item we're looking for. By doing this, we can compare things like prices, quality, features, and even customer reviews.

For example, let's say you want to buy a new toy. Instead of buying the first one you see, take some time to visit different stores or websites and see what they have to offer. Look at the prices and think about the quality and durability of the toy. You might even find that some places offer discounts or special deals.

Comparison shopping allows us to make sure we're getting the best value for our money. Sometimes, we might find that one store sells the same toy for a lower price, or another store offers better customer service. It's like putting together all the puzzle pieces and finding the perfect fit.

By comparing different options, we can also avoid impulse buying. It's important to take a step back, think about our needs and priorities, and make a decision that aligns with them. This helps us make wise choices and avoid regretting our purchases later.

Remember, comparison shopping is not just about finding the cheapest option. It's also about finding the best balance of quality, price, and value. It's like finding the perfect piece to complete a puzzle – it might take a little more time and effort, but it's worth it in the end.

So, next time you want to buy something, take the time to compare different options. Ask questions, read reviews, and make an informed decision. This way, you will show your children and grandchildren that you are a smart shopper and make the most of your hard-earned money.

Every dollar saved is a dollar less that needs to be earned.

Comparison shopping fosters smart consumer habits that will benefit your children throughout their lives. However, it is not always about price. It could be about quality, durability, and time as well. Either way, options should be chosen with benefits understood and realized.

Notes:

....

....

....

Money Fact: Australia and some other countries have specially designed bank notes that have raised dots on them to help the visually impaired distinguish between different denominations.

Chapter 4.

How Would Parents Describe the Term Opportunity Cost with Examples and Its Importance?

When explaining the concept of opportunity cost to children, a parent can use relatable examples to help them understand the concept and its importance. Here's how a grandparent might describe it:

Opportunity Cost is a fascinating concept that helps us make decisions in life. Imagine you have some money saved up, and you're trying to decide between buying a new toy or saving it for something else you want in the future. That's where opportunity cost comes into play.

Opportunity cost is the idea that when we choose to do or buy one thing, we give up the opportunity to do or buy something else. In simpler terms, it's about understanding that when we make a choice, there are other things we're giving up in return. It's like a trade-off.

For example, imagine you have $10, and you really want to buy a new video game. However, you also have the opportunity to save that money for a future family outing or to buy a special gift for someone you love. If you decide to spend the $10 on the video game, the opportunity cost would be giving up the chance to use that money for the family outing or the special gift.

Understanding opportunity cost helps us make better decisions because it encourages us to think about the value of our choices and what we might be sacrificing. It reminds us to consider the alternatives and weigh the benefits and drawbacks.

By considering opportunity cost, we become more aware of the consequences of our decisions. It helps us prioritize our wants and needs, and it teaches us the importance of making thoughtful choices that align with our goals and values.

Opportunity cost is a valuable concept that extends beyond just money. It applies to our time, energy, and other resources as well. It helps us become mindful of the choices we make and encourages us to think about the long-term impact of our decisions.

So, as your children grow older, they should continually consider the alternatives, weigh up the benefits and drawbacks, and make decisions that align with what's truly important to them. By understanding opportunity cost, they will become wise decision-makers and make the most of the opportunities that come their way.

Understanding opportunity cost empowers children to make thoughtful decisions throughout their lives, enabling them to prioritize their choices, and consider the value of their actions.

Notes:

....

....

....

Money Fact: In some regions of Bangladesh, mobile banks operate on boats, providing banking services to people in remote areas.

Chapter 5.

Why is Delayed Gratification Important and How Can Parents Explain it?

Delayed gratification is an important concept to teach children because it helps them develop self-discipline, patience, and the ability to prioritize long-term goals over immediate desires. It is the ability to resist the temptation of immediate rewards for future greater rewards or benefits.

Here's an example of how a parent might explain the importance of delayed gratification:

Imagine you have a plate of cookies in front of you, and they smell delicious. It's tempting to eat them all at once because they taste so good. But what if I told you that if you wait and don't eat them right away, I will give you two plates of cookies instead of one? You would have even more cookies to enjoy later!

I am sure you have heard the old story of "I will give you $1 million dollars right now or will give you a penny that doubles each day for 30 days." Which would you take?

Delayed gratification is about making a choice to wait for something better or more rewarding. It means having the patience and self-control to resist immediate pleasures for greater rewards in the future. When we practice delayed gratification, we learn to prioritize what truly matters to us and make thoughtful decisions.

In life, we often have to make choices between instant gratification and long-term benefits. For example, if you have some money, you can spend it on a toy right away or save it to buy something bigger and more special later on. By saving and waiting, you will be able to afford something even more exciting or important in the future.

Delayed gratification helps us become more responsible and successful. It teaches us to set goals, make sacrifices, and work towards achieving them. It helps us develop patience, perseverance, and the ability to resist impulsive decisions. It's like planting a seed and waiting for it to grow into a beautiful flower or a delicious fruit.

Remember, life is full of opportunities, and sometimes the best things come to those who wait. So, practice patience, think about your long-term goals, and choose delayed gratification. You'll be surprised by how much more you can achieve and enjoy in the future.

The benefits of delayed gratification help children understand the value of patience and making choices that could lead to greater rewards in the long run.

Notes:

....

....

....

Money Fact: A $20 gold coin called the Double Eagle made in 1933 was sold for over $7.5 million in a private transaction.

Chapter 6.

Why is Cash Flow Important?

Cash flow is important because it represents the movement of money into and out of a person's or organization's accounts. It reflects the inflow and outflow of cash over a specific period of time. Just as oxygen is crucial for sustaining life, cash flow is essential for the health and sustainability of an individual's finances. Here's an analogy that a parent might use to explain the relationship between cash flow and oxygen:

Imagine that your body needs oxygen to function properly. Oxygen is what keeps us alive and allows us to do all the things we love, like playing, running, and exploring. Without oxygen, our bodies wouldn't be able to survive and thrive.

In a similar way, cash flow is like oxygen for our personal finances. It's the lifeblood that keeps everything running smoothly. Cash flow is the money that comes into our accounts, such as income from our jobs, allowances, or any other sources. It's also the money that goes out, like expenses for groceries, bills, and other things we need to pay for.

Just as our bodies need a steady supply of oxygen to stay healthy and active, we need a steady flow of cash to keep things running smoothly. Without enough cash coming in, it becomes difficult to meet our needs and take care of our financial obligations. It's like trying to run without enough oxygen – we would quickly feel exhausted and struggle to keep going.

Cash flow allows us to pay for the things we need, save for the future, and even invest in opportunities that can help us grow. When our cash flow is healthy, it provides us with the freedom and flexibility to make choices and pursue our goals.

So, it's important to understand and manage our cash flow effectively. We need to make sure that we have enough money coming in to cover our expenses and have some left over for savings and emergencies. Just like breathing in oxygen and exhaling carbon dioxide, we want to ensure a healthy cycle of money coming in and going out.

By managing our cash flow wisely, we can maintain financial stability, seize opportunities, and create a solid foundation for a secure and fulfilling future.

Alternatively, when discussing cash flow, you can explain that money owed to you is not money that can be in the here and now. For example, if you are owed money for a completed chore but haven't received the money yet, you cannot buy candy from the store.

Children need to understand how vital cash flow is and the importance also for having some money in reserve through saving and not having the impulse to spend all that they have as soon as they receive it.

Notes:

....

....

....

Money Fact: "Money doesn't grow on trees" is a popular saying. A lot of bank notes are made from cotton and linen fibers, however in some parts of the world, some bank notes are made from a type of plastic.

Chapter 7.

How Can Parents Suggest Ways to Improve Cash Flow?

When suggesting ways to improve cash flow to their children, parents can offer practical advice and strategies that promote responsible money management. Here are a few suggestions:

1. **Budgeting**: Encourage your children to create a budget to track their income and expenses. This will show them when they receive their money and identify expenses that they are committed to and what they have available to spend. In other words – where is their money going? This may prompt discussion on where it is going and ways they can reduce spending or increase their income.

2. **Saving**: Have a conversation about the importance of saving money regularly through setting aside a portion of their income for emergencies and future goals. This will encourage them to prioritize saving before spending.

3. **Wise Spending**: Teach them to make wise spending choices by differentiating between needs and wants and by finding alternative options – new versus used, branded versus non branded, buy verses borrow (library books for

example). It is also important to encourage them to consider value and quality also when making purchasing decisions. Depending on the item, buying cheap could mean paying twice.

4. **Avoid Debt**: It is critical that parents discuss ways to avoid debt with older kids, especially when they receive or are offered their first credit card or store card. Discussing the pitfalls of debt and the importance of avoiding unnecessary borrowing will save them a lot of money and stress in the future. Ultimately, they need to know that it is not FREE money and there are financial dangers of high-interest rates and the long-term impact of debt on cash flow.

5. **Increase Income**: Encourage your children to explore opportunities to earn additional income. This can include part-time jobs, freelance work, or starting small businesses like selling crafts or offering services in their community. Along with extra money, this also helps instill a good work ethic, develop communication skills, and ultimately gain work experience that future employers seek.

6. **Negotiation Skills**: It doesn't hurt to ask for a discount or ultimately seek out offers and coupons when planning for or making a purchase. Any money saved is less money that

needs to be earned and it is also a way of maintaining a positive cash flow.

7. **Reduce Expenses**: In order to reduce expenses, help your children identify areas where costs can be cut. This could include controlling impulse purchases (at the checkout when about to pay at the store), taking a packed lunch, eating before going out etc. Remember the old adage to never go shopping on an empty stomach! In a family situation, finding ways to save on utilities, groceries, gas and so on can make a huge impact on cash flow.

8. **Smart Shopping**: By teaching them to compare prices, use coupons, and shop for discounts you will help your children save money, which is a fantastic life skill to develop as they go into adulthood regarding insurance, mortgages, internet etc. Showing them how to make informed decisions when shopping for goods and services will save a lot of money for them.

9. **Entrepreneurial Skills**: By encouraging your children to develop entrepreneurial skills and explore opportunities to generate income through creative means, you are also teaching them to problem solve, adapt and be more independent.

10. **Seek Financial Education**: As your children grow and evolve through their stages of life, they should be encouraged to learn more about personal finance through books, online resources, or courses. This will empower them to make informed financial decisions and improve their cash flow management skills.

By providing guidance and teaching practical strategies, parents can help their children improve their cash flow and develop a strong foundation for financial success.

Notes:

....

....

....

Money Fact: Approximately 38 million bank notes are produced daily by the US. Bureau of Engraving and Printing for a total of approximately $451 million.

Chapter 8.

How Can Parents Introduce Budgeting and Decision-Making Skills?

Parents can play a crucial role in introducing budgeting and decision-making skills to their children. Here are some strategies to help parents facilitate this process:

1. **Open Communication**: It is very important to be open and non-judgmental regarding money with your children. By encouraging them to ask questions, share their thoughts, and express their financial goals or concerns, you will help broaden their knowledge and address financial issues sooner rather than later. Although money is supposedly a simple concept, children need to understand that we all make mistakes. Ultimately by having open communication, you will create lifelong conversations about money.

2. **Set Financial Goals**: Helping your children set both short-term and long-term financial goals can be particularly advantageous. These goals can be related to saving for a specific item, contributing to a college fund, or starting a small business. By teaching children how to break down goals into manageable steps, you are teaching them how to create plans to achieve their financial goals. Allowing them

to see how goal setting is done, is different than simply suggesting that they should set goals.

3. **Allowance and Budgeting**: If you provide your children with an allowance, use it as an opportunity to teach budgeting skills. Encourage them to allocate their money into different categories such as savings, spending, and giving. Help them create a budget and track their expenses to develop an understanding of income and expenditures. Quite often they will amaze themselves by seeing where they have spent their money, and it will dawn on them why they never have money. This is a great start to discussing ways to spend less and keep track of their money.

4. **Financial Decision-Making**: Engage your children in discussions about financial decision-making. Present them with different scenarios and ask them to think critically about the best course of action. Encourage them to consider the pros and cons, evaluate the consequences, and make informed choices.

5. **Teach Wise Spending Habits**: Guide your children on making wise spending decisions. Discuss the importance of distinguishing between needs and wants, comparing prices, and seeking value for money. Help them understand the concept of delayed gratification and encourage them to

think about the long-term benefits of saving instead of impulse buying.

6. **Involve Them in Household Budgeting**: If appropriate, involve your children in discussions about household budgeting. Explain how you prioritize expenses, make financial decisions, and manage the family's finances. This provides them with real-life examples and gives them insights into budgeting practices. This may also help them in the future when they eventually leave home.

7. **Financial Literacy Resources**: Share age-appropriate financial literacy resources with your children. This can include books, articles, games, videos, or interactive online tools that teach basic financial concepts. Encourage them to explore these resources independently and discuss what they've learned. The discussions and conversations at the end are often the most important as they will gain a better understanding and how it will potentially be related to them now or in the future.

8. **Role Modeling**: Be a positive financial role model for your children. Demonstrate responsible money management habits, such as budgeting, saving, and making informed financial decisions. Show them how you prioritize needs, make thoughtful purchases, and save for the future. Your actions can leave a lasting impression and influence their

own financial behaviors. Remember you are also being observed which becomes learned behavior.

9. **Provide Guidance and Support**: Offer guidance and support whenever your children face financial challenges or have questions. Be available to discuss their concerns, offer advice, and help them navigate financial situations. Your wisdom and experience can provide valuable insights and help them develop critical thinking skills.

Money is a simple concept that is often overthought and made more complicated than it actually is. There are many aspects to our lives that can be related to money. Be open, honest and encourage discussions whenever you can. The more discussions, the easier it becomes to talk about (plus gives you more to talk to your child about). If you know more about their finances, the easier it is to guide them and to instill good money habits and skills that they can take forward. If they know they can come to you without judgement, then they are more likely to confide in you. Remember you are being observed and lot of what they see and do is learned.

Notes:

....

....

....

Money Fact: On the top left-hand corner of a US $10 bill, you can find a tiny owl hidden if you look close enough.

Chapter 9.

How Do You Create Hands-On Experiences with Regards to Money Management and Your Children?

Creating hands-on experiences for children to learn about money management is a valuable way to reinforce financial concepts and skills. Here are some ideas to help you create engaging hands-on experiences:

1. **Allowance and Budgeting**: Provide your children with a regular allowance and help them create a budget. Teach them to allocate money for different purposes, such as savings, spending, and giving. Encourage them to track their expenses and adjust their budget as needed.

2. **Savings Jar or Piggy Bank**: Give your children physical savings jars or piggy banks where they can deposit their money. Let them see the accumulation of their savings over time. Discuss the importance of saving for short-term and long-term goals. If they are old enough to have their own bank account, provide them with access to their own bank account so that they can see their money flowing into and out of their account and their current checking and savings balances. This is a great way to start a chat about savings, spending and money received.

3. **Play Money and Cash Register**: Use play money and a toy cash register to create a pretend store or marketplace at home. Help your children practice counting and making change (such a valuable skill). Teach them about the value of different denominations and the concept of paying for items with different denominations. This will massively help them with their multiplication, adding, subtraction and division skills.

4. **Grocery Shopping**: Take your children grocery shopping and involve them in the process. Give them a budget and let them help you make choices based on prices, discounts, and needs. Discuss the importance of comparing prices and making informed purchasing decisions. Along with prices you could also look at price per unit and the value of the clearance shelf items, too. Perhaps you challenge your children to find a list of items under a certain budget. You can then reduce the amount of money available and see if they can come up with alternatives. This is a great way to introduce budgeting.

5. **Entrepreneurship**: Encourage your children to start a small business, such as a lemonade stand, pet sitting service, or handmade crafts. Help them develop a plan, set prices, and track their income and expenses. This experience teaches them about earning money, managing

costs, and making a profit (not to mention building confidence, communication, and planning skills).

6. **Savings Challenges**: Set up savings challenges or goals for your children to achieve. For example, challenge them to save a certain amount of money in a specific timeframe and as a reward offer to match their savings contributions. Offer small rewards or incentives to motivate them and celebrate their achievements. Children and adults always "want" something, and it is important to learn to save to meet their "wants".

7. **Bank Visits**: Take your children to visit a bank or credit union. Help them understand the different services banks offer, such as savings accounts, checking accounts, and ATM usage. Show them how deposits and withdrawals work and explain the role of a bank in managing money. This is also a great way to introduce vocabulary that they may see in the bank or that they see on TV and will prompt their curiosity.

8. **Financial Board Games**: Play board games that involve money management and financial decision-making, such as CashCrunch Junior, Monopoly, The Game of Life, or Payday. These games simulate real-life financial scenarios and can help teach your children about budgeting, investing, and risk-taking. Board games also help develop other future life skills such as strategy, understanding the rules, patience,

adaptability, communication and being a humble winner and losing with integrity and humbleness.

9. **Online Resources and Apps**: Explore educational websites and apps specifically designed to teach kids about money management. Many interactive tools and games are available that cover topics like saving, budgeting, and basic financial literacy.

10. **Family Discussions**: Engage in regular family discussions about money-related topics. Share your own financial experiences, challenges, and successes. Encourage your children to ask questions and contribute to the conversation. This creates a supportive and open environment for learning.

By providing hands-on experiences, you are empowering your children to develop not only financial, but life skills while fostering a lifelong habit of responsible money management.

Notes:

....

....

....

A great activity for you to try:

If you have a Monopoly game in your house or have access to one, using the money, do the following:

Count out how much money comes into the household (this can be a rounded up or fictional amount). Then distribute the money between all the bills (mortgage, car, utilities, internet, groceries, taxes, insurance etc.) that are currently being paid including the allowances of the children if applicable. Your children now know where the money earned is going. If the children want more money for something, you can now ask them where it comes from. Just sit back and let them give you solutions and hold them to it (turning lights off, not wasting food...)

Money Fact: During World War II, the US. government changed the way they made pennies from copper to steel as a way of saving copper for use in the war.

Chapter 10.

How Can You Demonstrate Saving and Budgeting Practices to your Children?

To effectively demonstrate saving and budgeting practices to children, consider the following strategies:

1. **Create a Savings Jar**: Set up a visible savings jar or container where you can physically deposit money. Explain to your children that this is a designated place to save money for a specific goal, such as buying a toy or going on a special outing. Let them see the jar filling up over time to visually illustrate the progress of saving. This is also a great opportunity to help them connect the dots between the action (I am saving) and the result (I have saved).

2. **Set a Family Budget**: Involve your children in discussions about the family budget to help them understand that there is only so much money and that everything costs money. To prove this, you could get them to create a list of all the things in your household that cost money and over time make note of the costs (specific groceries, toiletries, games, toys, clothes etc.). Perhaps also help them understand that whenever a meal is wasted, lights are left on, and excessively long showers are taken, money is wasted. If money is being paid for the wasted food, lights being left

etc., it is taking away from what could be spent on rewards and treats. To understand the money aspect, budgets are used. Budgets help track income and expenses and ensure that money is allocated wisely. What financial goals (vacation, birthday gifts etc.) could you as parents and your children "work" together to achieve? *See previous Monopoly money exercise at the end of Chapter 9.*

3. **Use Envelopes or Digital Budgeting Apps**: Use envelopes or a digital budgeting app to allocate money for different categories, such as savings, groceries, entertainment, and more. Involve your children in the process by assigning them a category and allowing them to see how money is distributed and spent accordingly. This could be finding out how much electricity, water, internet, or groceries cost. With this knowledge, perhaps your children can work with you (hoping that they suggest solutions) to reduce the costs and wastage so that financial goals are met.

4. **Make Saving a Game**: Turn saving into a fun and engaging activity. Create a savings challenge where you challenge your children to compete to see who can save the most money within a certain timeframe. Use a chart to track progress and celebrate milestones together. Consider offering small rewards or incentives to make it more exciting. Creating a chart helps apply math that they have learned in their classes, which now becomes even more relevant as it is about them.

5. **Practice Smart Shopping**: Take your children grocery shopping and explain how to compare prices, look for discounts or coupons, and make smart choices. Discuss the difference between wants and needs and demonstrate how to make thoughtful decisions based on budgetary considerations. Does that mean purchasing or considering generic labels, clearance, bulk purchases etc.? This is a great time to introduce opportunity cost in terms of the advantages and disadvantages of choice.

6. **Encourage Goal Setting**: Help your children set short-term and long-term savings goals. For example, they might want to save a certain amount of money to buy a toy or save for a bigger goal like a bike or a trip. Break down the goals into smaller, achievable steps, and regularly check in on progress to keep them motivated.

7. **Share Personal Stories**: Share personal stories about your own experiences with saving and budgeting. Talk about times when you had to save for something you really wanted or had to make choices based on a budget. This will help your children understand that saving and budgeting are common practices and that everyone needs to make financial decisions.

8. Involve Them in Financial Decision-Making: Include your children in age-appropriate financial decisions. When planning a family outing or making a purchase, discuss the options, costs, and trade-offs involved. Encourage them to share their thoughts and consider their input. This helps them develop critical thinking skills and understand the decision-making process. What is the opportunity cost?

9. Reinforce Delayed Gratification: Teach your children the value of delayed gratification by demonstrating that saving for something special can be more rewarding than impulse buying. Encourage them to think about their purchases and consider waiting to see if they still want or need it later. This helps develop patience and reduces impulsive spending. How many toys and clothes that were "wanted" and bought, have not been used? Was the purchase a waste of money? How could the money have been used differently – spent on something else? Saved? Invested?

10. Celebrate Achievements: When your children reach a savings goal or demonstrate responsible budgeting behavior, celebrate their achievements. Acknowledge their efforts, praise their discipline, and offer words of encouragement. Celebrating milestones reinforces positive financial habits and motivates them to continue practicing saving and budgeting.

By involving your children in saving and budgeting practices from an early age, you are laying the foundation for their financial well-being and helping them develop lifelong skills.

Notes:

....

....

....

Money Fact: In the US, green ink was used in the printing process of money and that is where the term "greenback" came from.

Chapter 11.

How Might Parents Explain That Their Children Should Save Money Before They Spend?

When explaining to children the importance of saving before spending, simple and relatable stories can convey the concept effectively. For example:

"Imagine you have a jar of delicious candies, and you want to make sure you have enough to enjoy them for a long time. You know that if you eat all the candies right away, they will be gone, and you won't have any left for later. So, what you can do is save some of the candies in another jar before you start eating them. That way, you will always have a little stash of candies for later, even when the ones you eat right away are gone.

Just like candies, money works in a similar way. When you receive some money, it's tempting to spend it all right away on things that you want. But if you save a portion of it before spending, you create your own special stash of money. This saved money can be used for important things later, like buying something really special or even for unexpected situations that might come up. Saving before spending helps us feel secure and prepared for the future.

It's like building a little treasure chest of money that grows over time. By saving first, we make sure we have enough for the things we truly need or really want. So, whenever you receive money, remember to set aside a portion to save before using the rest. It's a smart habit that will help you feel more in control and ready for whatever comes your way."

So, in real terms. For every dollar that is received, save 10 cents, and put it as soon as you can into a savings jar. That way the money builds up over time which can then be changed into bank notes at a later date. On a personal note, over a 5-year span, I put all my spare change (dimes, nickels, and pennies) into a savings jar and had enough for a lawn mower! When my savings jar was full, I went to a coin machine in a supermarket and cashed in my coins. (When using a coin machine, always opt for the gift card equivalent as no commission is taken.)

If you save a little often, you get used to having a little less money, but can adapt your spending accordingly.

By emphasizing the benefits of saving, parents can help their children understand the concept and possibly slow their impulse to spend down, making smarter money decisions moving forward and ultimately growing their money.

Notes:

....

....

....

Money Fact: In the United Kingdom, 90 million coins are produced each day, which is more than the number of McDonald's hamburgers sold around the world.

Chapter 12.

How Do Parents Tell Their Children to Save and What Are Some Ways to Do It?

When parents want to encourage their children to save, they can approach the topic in a supportive and practical manner.

Saving means setting aside a portion of your money for the future, and it's a habit that can help you achieve your dreams and goals. I always like to use the mantra: "Save first, before you spend."

Here are some conversational tips to help your children begin their savings journey:

1. **Set a goal**: "Think about something you really want, like a new toy, a special outing, or even saving for a bigger purchase down the road. Having a set $$ goal in mind will give you something to work toward and motivate you to save."

2. **Make a plan**: "Decide how much money you want to save and how often. It can be a small amount each week or month, whatever works best for you. You can even create a

savings chart to track your progress and celebrate each milestone along the way."

3. **Save your gifts and allowances**: "Whenever you receive money as a gift or an allowance, try to save a portion of it. It might be tempting to spend it all at once, but by saving, you'll be building up your savings and having money available for other things later. If you put the money in the bank or invest it, you are making your money work for you."

4. **Separate spending and saving**: "Consider having two separate piggy banks or jars—one for spending and one for saving. This way, you can see your savings grow, and it will be easier to resist the urge to spend it all."

5. **Look for opportunities to earn money**: "Think about small jobs or tasks you can do to earn extra money. It could be helping with chores around the house, walking neighbors' dogs, or even selling crafts or baked goods. The more you earn, the more you can save. Plus, it improves your cash flow and maintains your savings and spending balances".

6. **Learn to prioritize**: "Sometimes, you might want to buy something right away, but it's important to think about whether it's a true need or something you can save for later.

In other words, do you really want it? Delaying gratification and making thoughtful choices will help you become a smarter saver."

"Remember, saving is not about missing out on fun or the things you enjoy. It's about being responsible, planning for the future, and having the freedom to do the things you love.."

"Saving is a lifelong skill that will serve you well, and I'm excited to see how your savings grow over time. Together, let's embark on this savings adventure and make your dreams come true!"

Although with young children you are asking them to save a dime and place it in a savings jar and save for a toy. Fast forward to adulthood, the same principle could mean saving for a deposit on a house or a car, or even investing and setting themselves up for financial independence. The concept is the same, just a difference in the amounts considered.

Notes:

....

....

....

Money Fact: The first paper money used was in China over 1000 years ago.

Chapter 13.

How Do You Instill into Children the Habit of Saving?

Instilling the habit of saving in children requires a consistent and intentional approach. Here are some strategies to help you:

1. **Lead by Example**: Children learn best through observation. Be a positive role model by practicing saving habits yourself. Let your child see you saving money, whether it's through a piggy bank or a savings account. Talk openly about your saving goals and how you make choices to save. Quite often there is a disconnect between earning the money, saving, and spending it. Apparently, money grows on trees and is in unlimited supply!

2. **Start Early**: Begin introducing the concept of saving as soon as your children are able to understand basic concepts. For keep a jar in the kitchen and show them that you put your lose change in there and write a savings goal amount on the jar. They now are able to connect the dots between putting coins in your savings jar and actually saving towards a goal.

3. **Set Savings Goals**: Help your children set specific savings goals, whether it's buying a toy, saving for a family outing, or contributing to a long-term goal like college or a special trip. Break down the goal into manageable increments and track progress together. This is a great way to start conversations about what amount that they need to save, and how they are going to do it. Also keeps everyone accountable and prompts discussions. Especially if each child has their own savings goal and amount that is needed to be saved. Nothing like sibling rivalry.

4. **Use Visual Aids**: Utilize visual aids, such as a savings jar or a chart, to help your children visualize their savings and growth. Seeing the actual progress being made can be motivating and rewarding for your children. Perhaps a chart, graph or a countdown number for example could be used.

5. **Offer Incentives**: Consider providing small incentives or rewards for reaching savings milestones. These could be special treats or activities that your children enjoy. However, be mindful not to create a dependency on these rewards, as the goal is to help your children learn to save for themselves without any need for motivation or free rewards from anyone else.

6. **Make Saving Fun**: Turn saving into a game or a challenge. For example, have a "saving race" where your children see

who can save the most money within a set period of time. Perhaps create a savings challenge or competition within the family to make it engaging and exciting. Along with money saved from their allowance, they could also add to their savings extra jobs completed on top of their chores and money saved from their actions like turning off lights, shorter showers, finishing their meals etc. This is a great way to save money around the house and again will create a conversation. Not to mention the number of extra jobs that will be completed around the house, giving everyone in the house extra time to enjoy a family day.

7. **Teach Delayed Gratification**: Help your children understand the concept of delayed gratification by encouraging them to save for something they really want instead of spending money impulsively. Discuss the value of waiting and how it can lead to greater satisfaction when they eventually reach their savings goal. Your children just need to do an audit of their rooms and around the house of things that have been bought that have hardly been used. What was the cost of the item and how many times did they use that item. If they had to buy it, based on their weekly allowance. How long would it take to purchase that item? Was it worth it to them?

8. **Involve Them in Budgeting**: Give your children opportunities to be part of family financial discussions, such as planning a budget for a family outing or grocery

shopping. This helps them understand the value of money and the importance of making thoughtful spending decisions. If they know how much money is available, it is easier to comprehend value and spending. By them knowing the amount, a game can be played to make that money last longer through smarter money decisions.

9. **Encourage Earning Opportunities**: Foster a sense of responsibility and ownership by offering opportunities for your children to earn money tasks or chores. This not only teaches them the value of hard work but also provides funds that they can learn to manage and ultimately save. Whether it is helping around the house, mowing the lawn, washing the cars, recycling etc. there is always something that they can do if they want extra money, but it must add value to the home. To add to that work ethic, you could also stipulate the quality of outcome factor. Thereby teaching that a good job will be rewarded. A bad job will not, which could affect earning potential and therefore savings. Which translates into general work ethic and future employment.

10. **Celebrate Milestones**: For most of us being told that we have done a good job is a great feeling. It doesn't take much effort to do but can have an everlasting impact on your child, their outcomes and memories. A child's learning curve is steep, and this is a great way to build confidence, that will spread into all other areas of their life. By celebrating and acknowledging your children, not just in

sports, school achievements etc., but also in their money habits and their savings achievements will make a huge difference. This reinforces the positive behavior and motivates them to continue saving, which ultimately will mean that they are preparing and are in training to save for their first car or deposit on a house.

Be patient and supportive. Encourage and reflect on the benefits and rewards of saving. By instilling this habit early on, you are equipping them with a valuable life skill that will serve them well into adulthood.

Notes:

....

....

....

Money Fact: The first official coins for the US were made in 1793.

Chapter 14.

How Do Parents Explain Compound Interest to Their Children?

Explaining compound interest to children can help them understand the power of saving and investing over time. Here's an example of how a parent might explain compound interest:

"Imagine having a magical piggy bank that grows money all by itself. This happens when you put money in your piggy bank, and it starts to grow really quickly. A bit like in the fairytale story of Jack and the Beanstalk where the 3 beans were magical and caused the beanstalk to grow really quickly compared to other beams. Using that same analogy, we can say that there is something called compound interest that can cause savings to grow really quickly. It does this by growing the money over and over again."

Let's say you put $10 in your piggy bank, and it earns 10% interest every year. At the end of the first year, you would have $11 because you earned $1 in interest. But here's the magical part: In the second year, you don't just earn interest on your original $10, but also on the $1 you earned in interest making it $11. So, you would earn $1.10 in interest, making your total $12.10.

As time goes on, your piggy bank keeps growing faster and faster because it earns interest not only on your original money but also on the interest it earns. The more money you save and the longer you keep it in your piggy bank, the more it will grow through the power of compound interest.

Compound interest is like a snowball rolling down a hill. It starts small, but as it rolls and collects more snow, it becomes bigger and bigger. Similarly, your savings can grow over time if you keep adding to it and let the power of compound interest work its magic.

This is why it's important to start saving early and regularly. Even small amounts can add up over time thanks to compound interest. By putting your money to work and letting it grow, you can reach your goals faster and have more financial security in the future.

So, whenever you have some money to spare, think about putting it in your magical piggy bank. Watch it grow and see how your savings can help you achieve your dreams and make your future brighter."

Just a disclaimer, unless you are going to match your child's savings, it is actually best to put it into a bank or some kind of financial institution for their money to grow.

Unfortunately, the same can happen for credit card debt, where interest is paid on the original amount and the interest being charged, making debt very expensive.

Magical piggy banks and snowballs are just two relatable examples that can be used to highlight the concept of growing money over time. It is very important that parents help their children grasp the concept of compound interest and the benefits of saving and investing for the long term because ultimately it is free money.

Notes:

....

....

....

Money Fact: A long time ago money used to be stored in pots before banks and other institutions were invented. The story goes that the pots were made of a certain type of clay called pygg. So, whenever people put extra coins into one of their clay jars, they put the coins into their pygg pot which later evolved to being called a piggy bank.

Chapter 15.

How Would Parents Explain Banking, Savings Accounts, Interest Rates and Assist Children in Opening Their Own Savings Accounts?

1. **Simplify the Concept**: Start by explaining the basic concept of banks as secure places where people deposit their money. Perhaps even mention the origins of the Piggy bank as mentioned in the previous chapter. Emphasize that banks help keep money safe and provide various financial services such as: checking accounts, savings accounts, investing accounts, bank loans and more.

2. **Introduce Savings Accounts**: Explain that a savings account is a type of bank account designed for individuals to deposit and save their money. Describe how savings accounts offer a safe place to store money while also earning interest over time.

3. **Discuss Interest**: Break down the concept of interest by explaining that it is the money earned on the amount saved in a bank account. Illustrate how interest helps money grow over time, allowing individuals to earn extra income from their savings. For example, for every dollar saved in a savings account, depending on the account (high interest), they could see returns of 5% (5 cents) on every dollar saved.

4. **Visit a Bank**: Take your children on a field trip to a local bank. Show them the different areas of the bank, such as the teller stations, ATMs, and customer service areas. Explain the role of each section and how they facilitate banking transactions. *Explain that in order to draw money out, they must first actually have money in the bank!*

5. **Demonstrate Transactions**: While at the bank, demonstrate a typical banking transaction such as depositing money or withdrawing cash. Explain the process step-by-step, from filling out a deposit slip or using an ATM to completing the transaction with a teller or machine. It is also very important to explain that when money is withdrawn, there is less available etc.

6. **Open a Savings Account**: If appropriate, assist your children in opening their own savings accounts. Research banks that offer special savings accounts for children or teenagers. Accompany them to the bank, help them fill out the necessary forms, and explain the importance of depositing money regularly.

7. **Track and Discuss Progress**: Encourage your children to regularly check their savings account balance and review their account statements. This is a great habit to get into while learning where their money is going and keeping up

to date with their financials. Discuss the impact of interest on their savings and how their money is growing over time. This helps them understand the benefits of saving and the power of compound interest.

8. **Set Savings Goals**: Help your children set savings goals for different purposes, such as buying a toy, saving for college, or donating to a charity. Guide them in creating a plan to achieve their goals and monitor their progress together. *A great way to save money for college is to open a 529 (for example). If it is a child's birthday, instead of getting a large number of presents, perhaps family members can contribute towards their college fund. You can find various 529 gift cards in stores.*

9. **Reinforce Saving Habits**: Encourage your children to develop a habit of saving by setting aside a portion of their allowance or any money they receive as gifts. Discuss the importance of saving regularly and making conscious decisions about spending and saving.

10. **Share Personal Stories**: Share personal stories about your own experiences with banks, savings accounts, and interest. Talk about how saving money helped you achieve financial goals or how interest played a role in growing your savings. These stories can make the concepts more relatable and engaging.

By explaining the various financial vehicles available to them such as banks, savings accounts, and interest to your children, you are empowering them with the knowledge and skills necessary to make informed financial decisions and develop healthy saving habits.

Notes:

....

....

....

Money Fact: The magnetic stripe on credit and debit cards was first introduced in the 1970s to make transactions faster and more secure.

Chapter 16.

How Can Parents Explain Taxes and Why They are Collected?

Explaining taxes to children can be a great opportunity for parents to teach their children about civic responsibility and the importance of contributing to society and the functioning of communities.

Taxes are a way that we contribute to our community and help support the things we all need and enjoy, like schools, roads, hospitals, and parks.

1. **What are taxes**: Taxes are a certain percentage of our income or the money we earn that we pay to the government. The government then uses that money to provide essential services and programs for everyone.

2. **Types of taxes**: There are different types of taxes. The most common ones are income tax, which is based on how much money we earn from working (or other sources), and sales tax, which is a small percentage added to the price of things we buy.

3. **How taxes help**: Taxes help fund important services and infrastructure that benefit everyone in our community. They help pay for things like public schools, libraries, parks, and public transportation. Taxes also support programs that assist people who may need help, such as healthcare, social services, and emergency services.

4. **Paying taxes**: When we work, the government takes a portion of our earnings as taxes. This happens automatically, and our employers deduct it from our paychecks. Other types of taxes, like sales tax, are added to the cost of things we buy when we make a purchase.

5. **Being a responsible citizen**: Paying taxes is a responsibility we have as citizens. It's our way of contributing to the well-being of our community and helping it grow and prosper. By paying taxes, we help ensure that everyone has access to important services and opportunities.

6. **The importance of honesty**: It's important to be honest when it comes to taxes. We should accurately report our income and pay the right amount of taxes based on what we earn. This helps maintain fairness and ensures that everyone contributes their fair share.

Taxes can seem complicated, but they are a necessary part of how our society functions. By paying our taxes, we are helping local government fund various public services and programs that benefit everyone in our community.

These benefits include:

1. **Funding public services**: Taxes are collected to finance essential public services that we all rely on. These include things like schools, hospitals, police and fire departments, roads and bridges, parks, libraries, and much more. By paying taxes, we help ensure that these important services are available to everyone.

2. **Building infrastructure**: Taxes are used to build and maintain infrastructure, such as roads, bridges, public transportation systems, and utilities. These infrastructure projects contribute to the development and well-being of our communities, making it easier for people to travel, access goods and services, and enjoy a higher quality of life.

3. **Supporting social programs**: Taxes are also used to fund social programs that help people in need. These programs might provide healthcare services, support for low-income families, assistance for the elderly or disabled, and other forms of social support. By paying taxes, we contribute to creating a safety net for those who require assistance.

4. **Ensuring fairness and equity**: Taxes play a crucial role in promoting fairness and equity in society. They help distribute the costs of running a country or community among its residents based on their ability to pay. This means that those who earn more or have more resources contribute a larger share of taxes, while those with lower incomes pay proportionally less.

5. **Civic responsibility**: Paying taxes is a civic responsibility we have as citizens. It's part of being an active participant in our society and contributing to the common good. By fulfilling our tax obligations, we are helping to support the institutions, services, and programs that make our communities thrive.

Understanding taxes and their impact is an important part of becoming an informed and responsible citizen.

On a side note, next time your child has an ice cream or a sandwich or a slice of pizza etc., take a bite and tell them it is their parent tax. Might start a conversation!

According to some, there are only two certainties in life – death and taxes and so it is important to understand why we are taxed and where and why our money is being taken from us and used. Open dialogue and addressing any questions or concerns will enhance the learning experience and foster a sense of civic responsibility. This could be a very interesting topic depending on who you talk to.

Notes:

....

....

....

Money Fact: Federal income tax was introduced in 1913 when the Sixteenth Amendment was signed, giving Congress the right to levy and collect income taxes.

Chapter 17.

Should Kids be Given an Allowance?

Whether or not to give kids an allowance is a personal decision that varies from family to family. If you choose to give your children an allowance, you will certainly want to have a conversation with them about how to manage their allowance. This conversation could include positive money saving habits and money management skills.

1. **Financial Responsibility**: Giving kids an allowance helps them learn financial responsibility from a young age. It allows them to manage their own money, make choices about spending and saving, and gain a better understanding of the value of money (especially when they are spending their own money). When the money is gone, it is gone. Children now learn that there is limited money and smarter choices need to be made next time so the money doesn't run out.

2. **Budgeting Skills**: An allowance can teach children how to budget and allocate their money effectively. They can learn to divide their allowance into different categories such as savings, spending, and giving, which promotes wise money management habits. They also learn that they will have to wait until their next allowance or possibly look to earn extra

income through completing extra jobs on top of their chores around the house.

3. **Decision-Making**: Having their own money gives kids the opportunity to make decisions and experience the consequences of their choices. They can learn to prioritize their spending, differentiate between needs and wants, and understand the trade-offs involved in financial decision-making.

4. **Independence and Empowerment**: Receiving an allowance can give kids a sense of independence and empowerment. It allows them to take ownership of their financial decisions, fostering confidence and self-reliance. The important part of this is to let them spend their money how they want to, rather than how you see fit. If they make a mistake, it is a much cheaper lesson than it could be later in life.

5. **Life Skills Development**: Managing an allowance teaches kids important life skills such as basic math, budgeting, critical thinking, and planning. These skills will be valuable as they grow older and face more complex financial situations.

6. **Financial Literacy**: An allowance provides an opportunity for parents to teach their children about financial concepts such as saving, budgeting, earning, and even investing. Parents can engage in conversations about money, imparting valuable financial knowledge and skills.

7. **Reward for Responsibilities**: Linking the allowance to certain responsibilities or chores can teach children the connection between effort and reward. It helps instill a work ethic and the understanding that money is earned through work and contribution.

Ultimately, the decision to give kids an allowance should be based on the family's values, financial situation, and parenting philosophy. It's important to use the allowance as a tool for teaching financial literacy and responsibility, rather than as a means of spoiling or enabling unhealthy spending habits. In the long term an allowance will help a child understand the value of money and if they make mistakes and waste their money early on, it is a very inexpensive lesson in the grand scheme of things.

Notes:

....

....

....

Money Fact: Allowances vary from 50c to $1 per week for each year of a child's age, with the average being $18 per week. 61% of families give their children allowances.

https://mint.intuit.com/blog/trends/average-allowances-in-america-by-age-0813-2/

Chapter 18.

What Do Parents Say About Peer Pressure, Branding and Consumerism?

When discussing peer pressure, branding, and consumerism with children, parents can offer valuable insights and advice. Here are some points parents might make:

1. **Individuality and Authenticity**: Encourage your children to embrace their unique qualities and interests. Explain that peer pressure often arises from a desire to fit in, but it's important for them to stay true to themselves and not be swayed by others' opinions or trends.

2. **Critical Thinking**: Teach your children to think critically about advertising and branding. Help them understand that companies use persuasive techniques to convince consumers to buy their products. Encourage them to question whether a product or brand truly aligns with their values and needs, rather than succumbing to the pressure of trends.

3. **Quality Over Popularity**: Emphasize the importance of considering the quality and functionality of a product over its popularity or branding. Teach them to make informed

decisions based on durability, value for money, and long-term benefits, rather than solely relying on the appeal of a brand.

4. **Financial Consequences**: Discuss the financial implications of impulsive purchases and the impact of consumerism (the pressure to purchase things) on personal finances. Help your children understand that constantly seeking the latest trends or succumbing to peer pressure can lead to unnecessary spending and financial stress.

5. **Advertising Tactics**: Teach your children to recognize common advertising tactics, such as emotional appeals, celebrity endorsements, or limited time offers. Explain that advertisers often create a sense of urgency or make products appear more desirable than they actually are. By understanding these tactics, your children can make more informed choices.

6. **Value of Experiences**: Shift the focus from material possessions to the value of experiences and relationships. Encourage your children to prioritize spending on experiences that create lasting memories and personal growth rather than simply accumulating material possessions.

7. **Delayed Gratification**: Help your children understand the concept of delayed gratification. Teach them to set goals, save money, and wait for things they truly desire. Explain that by practicing patience and self-control, they can make more meaningful and deliberate purchases. Revisit the idea of delayed gratification and the audit that you may or may not have done regarding purchases.

8. **Environmental Impact**: Discuss the impact of consumerism on the environment. Help your children understand the importance of sustainability and making conscious choices to reduce waste and preserve natural resources. Encourage them to support brands that prioritize eco-friendly practices. There are a lot of eco-friendly messages out there. Make sure you do your own research so that you can back up your own views. A "just because" is not an answer that people will take seriously.

9. **Setting Priorities**: Guide your children in setting financial priorities. Help them understand the importance of saving money for meaningful goals and the satisfaction that comes from achieving those goals rather than succumbing to instant gratification.

10. **Media Literacy**: Teach your children to be critical consumers of media. Help them understand that not everything they see or hear is accurate or beneficial.

Encourage them to seek diverse perspectives, fact-check information, and develop their own opinions rather than blindly accepting what is presented to them.

By addressing peer pressure, branding, and consumerism with your children, you can empower them to make informed choices, develop their own values, and resist the negative influences of materialism. The more conversations you have, the more it will help your child stand apart. If your child understands the value of money, they are less likely to be wasteful and bow to pressure. They might purchase an expensive item but will value it more as they have had to plan, budget and save for it.

Notes:

....

....

....

Money Fact: Teens spend on average $2600 on clothes and fast food.

https://teenfinancialfreedom.com/buying-habits-of-teenagers/

Chapter 19.

What are Credit Scores and How Can Parents Explain Them to Their Children?

Credit scores are numbers that reflect an individual's creditworthiness (the ability to manage debt). They are used by lenders, such as banks or credit card companies, to assess the risk of lending money to someone. Explaining credit scores to children can be done in a simplified and relatable manner. Here's an example:

Think of a credit score as a report card for your money habits. Just like your school report card shows how well you're doing in your classes; a credit score shows how well you handle your money and in particular debt. It's a number that tells others, like banks or lenders, whether you're good at paying back money you borrow.

When you want to borrow money, like getting a loan for a car or a credit card, lenders look at your credit score to decide if they should lend you the money. If you have a high credit score, it means you have a good track record of paying back what you owe on time. This makes lenders more likely to trust you and offer you better terms, like lower interest rates or higher loan amounts.

On the other hand, if you have a low credit score, it means you may have had some trouble in the past paying back money you borrowed. This could make lenders hesitant to lend you money or give you less favorable terms, like higher interest rates or lower loan amounts.

To have a good credit score, it's important to practice responsible money habits. This includes paying your bills on time (or even early), keeping your credit card balances low, and only borrowing money when you really need it. It's like doing well in your classes by studying, completing assignments, and being responsible.

Remember, your credit score is not only important when you want to borrow money, but it can also affect other things like renting an apartment or even getting a job. So, it's essential to be mindful of your money habits and build a good credit score from an early age.

It is also important to explain that when you use a credit card, you are borrowing money with the promise of paying it back within a certain time. If you do not, you will get charged a daily percentage rate on the amount that you borrowed and the outstanding interest. It can get very expensive. The amount compounds quickly and you will have to pay a lot more back. It is also important to understand that any interest paid means extra money must be earned to replace it.

Credit scores are probably one of the most misunderstood concepts out there, which unfortunately can have a devastating effect on your finances if misused. By comparing credit scores to a report card, parents can help their children understand the significance of credit scores and how responsible money habits play a role in maintaining a good credit score. It is very important to encourage your children to do further research on credit utilization, carrying balances and so on once they are ready to tackle those concepts.

Notes:

....

....

....

Money Fact: Credit cards in the US were originally introduced in the 1920s to loyal customers of certain companies and stores.

Chapter 20.

What Should Parents Say About Continual Learning and the Different Stages of Life?

When discussing continual learning and the different stages of life with children, parents can offer valuable wisdom and guidance. These conversations can not only have a positive impact on finances but improve the overall quality of life. Here are some points parents might make:

1. **Embrace Lifelong Learning**: Encourage your children to have a thirst for knowledge and a curiosity about the world. Explain that learning doesn't stop with formal education but continues throughout life. Emphasize the importance of being open to new experiences and constantly seeking opportunities to learn and grow.

2. **Adaptability and Resilience**: Share the importance of being adaptable and resilient in the face of life's changes and challenges. Explain that each stage of life presents unique opportunities and obstacles, and the ability to learn and adapt is crucial for personal growth and success.

3. **Learning from Mistakes**: Share stories of your own experiences and the lessons you learned from your mistakes. Encourage your children to embrace failure as a natural part of the learning process and emphasize the importance of resilience, self-reflection, and growth from setbacks.

4. **Emphasize Personal Development**: Discuss the significance of personal development and self-improvement. Encourage your children to set goals and work towards self-improvement in various aspects of life, such as relationships, career, hobbies, and personal well-being.

5. **Multiple Career Paths**: Share that there are multiple paths to success and fulfillment. Explain that it's common for people to have multiple careers or change career paths throughout their lives. Encourage your children to explore their passions and interests, and to be open to new opportunities that may arise in different stages of life.

6. **Pursue Passion and Purpose**: Encourage your children to find their passions and purpose in life. Help them understand that a fulfilling life comes from aligning their values, interests, and talents with their chosen path. Emphasize the importance of pursuing meaningful work and making a positive impact on others.

7. **Embrace Change and Growth**: Discuss the inevitability of change and growth in life. Help your children understand that personal growth often happens through stepping out of their comfort zones, embracing new experiences, and continuously learning from those experiences.

8. **Cherish Memories and Relationships**: Share the value of cherishing memories and nurturing relationships throughout life. Encourage your children to build meaningful connections with family, friends, and mentors. Explain that these relationships can provide support, guidance, and lifelong learning opportunities.

9. **Share Stories and Wisdom**: Share your own life experiences, lessons learned, and wisdom gained throughout the different stages of your life. Your stories can offer valuable insights and inspiration, helping your children navigate their own journeys.

10. **Be Present and Grateful**: Encourage your children to live in the present moment and cultivate gratitude for the experiences and opportunities they have. Remind them to appreciate each stage of life and the unique lessons it offers.

By instilling in your children a mindset of growth, an awareness of adaptability, and the importance of lifelong learning, you are setting them up for a healthy financial future. Your guidance can help them embrace change, seize opportunities, and navigate the complexities of life with wisdom and resilience. In our lifetime we have seen CD-ROMs transform into Blu-ray and dial up internet change into hotspot connections and more. Along with these changes, children will also go through their own stages of life where at first, they will be learning to save money in a piggy bank, later managing their checking accounts, then paying a mortgage followed by investing and looking into retirement funds.

Notes:

....

....

....

Money Fact: The average person will have 12 jobs in their lifetime.

https://www.zippia.com/advice/average-number-jobs-in-lifetime

Chapter 21.

How Can Entrepreneurship and Earning Money be Encouraged?

Entrepreneurship simply put means finding a business opportunity and exploiting it. Encouraging children to explore entrepreneurship and earn money can be an exciting and valuable learning experience. Here are some ways parents can inspire their children in this area:

1. **Foster Creativity and Passion**: Encourage your children to explore their interests, hobbies, and talents. Help them identify areas they are passionate about and guide them towards entrepreneurial opportunities related to those interests. YouTube, Crafting, Design are examples of some of the current opportunities you might discuss with your child.

2. **Brainstorm Business Ideas**: Sit down with your children and brainstorm potential business ideas together. Ask them questions that will spark their creativity and critical thinking. Help them think about what products or services they can offer and how they can stand out from the competition. Creative and critical thinking skills expand their thinking processes and ultimately enable children to think "outside of the box". This development of thinking

and problem-solving skills will help them stand out from the competition. Unfortunately, life is a competition whether we like it or not. As long as there are options, there is competition.

3. **Support the Development of Skills**: Identify skills that can be valuable in entrepreneurship, such as communication, problem-solving, marketing, or financial management. Encourage your children to develop these skills through books, online resources, workshops, and mentorship programs. You might even encourage your children to talk with adults in your circle or approach local business professionals that are working in area your children have an interest in pursuing. There are always people who want to help.

4. **Set Up a Lemonade Stand or Small Business**: Help your children set up a lemonade stand or assist them in starting a small business. Guide them in planning the business, creating a budget, setting prices, marketing their products or services, and handling transactions. This hands-on experience can teach them important entrepreneurial skills. Not only does learning take place with knowledge and understanding being gained, but relationships are being developed between you and your children and the community. Examples could be online Etsy stores, selling on eBay or even a joint venture between you both.

5. Mentorship and Guidance: Offer your knowledge and expertise as a mentor to your children. Share your own experiences with entrepreneurship or connect them with other entrepreneurs who can provide guidance and inspiration. Be available to answer their questions and provide ongoing support throughout their entrepreneurial journey. As previously mentioned, make introductions to adults who you may know who can speak to them about their aspirations and ideas. You never know, they may well be offered an internship/work experience or a part time job.

6. Teach Financial Literacy: Help your children understand the financial aspects of running a business. Teach them about budgeting, pricing, profit margins, and the importance of managing expenses. Introduce them to basic accounting concepts and involve them in tracking their income and expenses. It is also important for your children to understand that as they get older there are more financial concepts to learn and opportunities to grow their wealth as well as lose it if they are not careful.

7. Encourage Problem-Solving: Encourage your children to identify problems or challenges in their community or daily life and think of creative solutions. Help them understand that entrepreneurship is often about finding innovative ways to solve problems and meet the needs of others. This could be a daily game in where you spot something and ask whether it works well or could be improved and if so, how?

8. **Networking and Collaboration**: Teach your children the value of networking and collaboration. Help them connect with other young entrepreneurs or join local youth entrepreneurship programs or clubs. Encourage them to share ideas, learn from others, and collaborate on projects. This should also include etiquette for addressing people and dressing in a sense that will make great first impressions. On a personal note, I was once asked to speak in a business class in a high school. One of the students was very disrespectful throughout and would not take his feet off his desk. I had asked him to remove them but would not. At the end of my talk, he came to speak to me and ask if he could have a job. I did not even consider offering this student a job due to such a negative first impression.

9. **Celebrate and Reward Efforts**: Acknowledge and celebrate your children's entrepreneurial efforts, regardless of the outcome. Recognize their hard work, creativity, and determination. Reward their achievements, even if it's as simple as offering words of encouragement or treating them to a special experience. If it is a failure, there are some things that can be celebrated and other things that can be improved upon and tried again, which will eventually become a success. This also shows resilience and the need to try again. Success comes from determination.

10. **Emphasize the Learning Process**: Teach your children that entrepreneurship is not just about financial success but also about personal growth and learning from failures. Help them understand that setbacks and challenges are opportunities for growth and improvement. Encourage resilience and a growth mindset.

By encouraging your children to discover entrepreneurship and earn money, you are instilling them with important skills, such as creativity, problem-solving, financial literacy, and a strong work ethic. This will not only boost confidence but will help your children stand out as life is a competition and therefore have a greater chance of success. Although qualifications are valuable, it is often down to who you know, first impressions or that ability to think things through and perform under pressure.

Notes:

....

....

....

Money Fact: According to the US Business Formation Statistics, just over 5 million businesses applications were filed in 2022.

Chapter 22.

How Should Parents Answer Their Children's Questions and Encourage Their Ideas?

When children ask questions or share ideas about money, it is important for parents to create an open and supportive environment that encourages curiosity and learning. Here are some tips on how parents can effectively answer children's questions and encourage their ideas:

1. **Listen attentively**: Give your children your full attention when they ask questions or share their ideas about money. Show genuine interest and let them know that their thoughts and inquiries are valued. There is no such thing as a stupid question. If it is a question that they are asking, it is something that they do not know and want an answer.

2. **Respond with patience and clarity**: Use simple and age-appropriate language to explain financial concepts. Break down complex ideas into smaller, understandable parts. If you don't know the answer to a question, be honest and suggest you find the information together.

3. **Encourage critical thinking**: Instead of providing all the answers right away, encourage your children to think through each question and explore possible solutions. Ask

open-ended questions that promote critical thinking and problem-solving skills. This helps them develop their own ideas and reasoning abilities.

4. **Validate their ideas**: Even if your children's ideas about money may seem unconventional or different from your own, validate their perspectives. Let them know that their thoughts and opinions matter. Engage in discussions that allow them to express their ideas and provide a safe space for open dialogue.

5. **Share personal experiences**: Draw upon your own experiences with money to provide real-life examples and stories. This can help make financial concepts more relatable and easier to understand. Share both successes and challenges to provide a well-rounded view of money management.

6. **Empower them to find solutions**: Instead of always giving direct answers, encourage your children to find solutions on their own. Guide them towards resources like books, online articles, or educational websites where they can explore and learn more about financial topics. These are skills that they will rely on throughout life when it comes to lifelong learning.

7. **Support their curiosity**: If your children show a keen interest in a particular aspect of money, encourage them to pursue it further. Help them find books, games, or activities that align with their interests. This fosters a love for learning and allows them to explore their curiosity about money.

8. **Emphasize learning from mistakes**: Teach your children that making mistakes is a natural part of the learning process. Encourage them to see setbacks as opportunities for growth and learning. Share stories of your own financial mistakes and the lessons you learned from them. Perhaps you have had buyers' remorse. What did you learn from it?

9. **Foster creativity and entrepreneurship**: If your children express entrepreneurial ideas or show an interest in money-making ventures, support their creativity. Help them brainstorm ways to turn their ideas into reality. This can instill a sense of initiative, problem-solving skills, and financial independence.

10. **Be a supportive resource**: Let your children know that they can always turn to you for guidance and support. Offer to be a sounding board for their ideas, answer their questions, and provide ongoing encouragement as they continue to explore and learn about money.

Remember, every child is unique, and their curiosity about money may vary. Tailor your responses and engagement to their individual interests and abilities. By answering their questions and encouraging their ideas, you are fostering not only their curiosity, knowledge and understanding, but helping them with their financial literacy. You are also empowering them to become more confident and responsible money managers.

Notes:

....

....

....

Money Fact: 30% of teens in the US aged 16 to 19 have part time jobs while attending school.

https://www.zippia.com/advice/high-school-job-statistics/

Chapter 23.

How do Parents Teach Their Children about Scams?

The vast majority of people in the world who are connected online or run a household could be at risk of being scammed. Any type of information associated with financial, identity and/or medical details can be extremely valuable to people with bad intentions. With this information being so valuable, there are people out there who try to trick others and take their money or obtain personal information that they can sell. Here are a couple of pointers and conversations that can be shared.

1. **Be skeptical**: It's okay to question things that seem too good to be true. Scammers often promise quick and easy ways to make money or get rich, but remember, there's usually a catch. If something sounds too good to be true, it probably is.

2. **Guard your personal information**: Teach your children to never share personal information like their address, phone number or social security number with someone they don't know or trust. Scammers can use this information to steal their children's identity and cause problems.

3. **Think before you click**: Teach your children to be cautious when clicking on links or opening attachments in emails, text messages, or on social media. Scammers may try to trick them into giving them access to their computer or personal information. Tell your children that if they are unsure, always check with a trusted adult before clicking.

4. **Verify before you trust**: It's important that your children know to take a moment to verify a person's identity if someone contacts them claiming to be from a company or organization. They should hang up and call the official number or visit the official website of the company to check if it's a legitimate contact.

5. **Talk to a trusted adult**: Remind your children that if they receive any suspicious messages or encounter something that doesn't feel right, they should talk to a trusted adult family member or friend. The trusted adult can help and guide them in handling these situations.

Remember, it's not about living in fear, but about being smart and informed. By knowing about scams and staying vigilant, you can teach your children to protect themselves and others from falling victim to these schemes.

Perhaps, as a whole family, this would be a regular and worthwhile chat to have about how to protect each other.

By having an open and honest conversation, parents can equip their children with the knowledge and critical thinking skills needed to identify and avoid scams. It's important to establish a trusting relationship and let the child know they can always turn to a responsible adult for guidance and support.

Notes:

....

....

....

Money Fact: 1 in 10 adults in the US will fall victim to a scam or fraud every year. $2.7 billion was stolen by internet-enabled theft, fraud and exploitation. 1.3 million children have their identities stolen every year.

https://legaljobs.io/blog/scam-statistics/

Chapter 24.

How Do Parents Explain the Difference Between Scamming, Phishing, and Identity Theft?

Explaining the differences between scamming, phishing, and identity theft to children can help them understand the various tactics used by scammers. Here are a couple of pointers and conversations you can have.

1. **Scamming**: Scamming is when someone tries to deceive or trick others to steal their money or personal information. Scammers may use phone calls, emails, or even in-person approaches to convince people to give them money or sensitive details. They often make false promises or create fake situations to make their scam seem believable.

2. **Phishing**: Phishing is a type of scam that usually happens online. Scammers pretend to be a trustworthy organization, such as a bank, social media platform, or online store, and they send emails or messages that look real. They try to trick you into providing your personal information, like passwords or credit card details by creating a sense of urgency or by posing as someone you trust. Remember, legitimate organizations will never ask for sensitive information through email or messaging.

3. **Identity Theft**: Identity theft occurs when someone steals your personal information like your name, social security number, or bank account details with the intent to use it for fraudulent purposes. The thief may open credit cards in your name, make unauthorized purchases, or commit other crimes using your identity. It can be a serious and damaging crime, which is why it's important to protect your personal information.

To stay safe from scams, phishing, and identity theft, here are some tips to share with your children:

➢ Be cautious of unsolicited phone calls, emails, or messages from unknown sources.

➢ Never share personal information or financial details with someone you don't trust or didn't initiate contact with.

➢ Verify the authenticity of websites, emails, or messages by contacting the organization directly using official contact information.

➢ Keep your computer and devices secure by using strong passwords, installing reliable antivirus software, and keeping your software up to date.

- Regularly review your financial statements and credit reports for any suspicious activity.

Your children should be encouraged to share with you, or any trusted adult suspicious messages received or encounters that do not seem right, who can help them navigate these situations.

Being aware and informed is your best defense against scams and identity theft.

By explaining the differences between scamming, phishing, and identity theft in simple terms and providing practical tips, parents can empower their children to be vigilant and protect themselves in the digital age. Who knows, as we get older our children might be educating us on the latest scams and identity theft.

Notes:

....

....

....

Money Fact: The Federal Trade Commission (FTC) reported that more than 2.8 million consumers reported fraud to the value of over $2.3 billion in imposter scams.

https://www.ftc.gov/news-events/news/press-releases/2022/02/new-data-shows-ftc-received-28-million-fraud-reports-consumers-2021

Chapter 25.

How and Why Should Parents Share the Idea of Gifting and Charitable Behavior with Their Children?

Parents have a wonderful opportunity to teach their children about the value of gifting, charitable behavior and citizenship. Here's how and why they can share this important concept:

1. **Lead by example**: Show your children the joy of giving by engaging in charitable activities yourself. Share stories of how you have helped others or volunteered your time and encourage them to join you in these endeavors. By being a role model, you inspire them to follow in your footsteps.

2. **Explain the impact**: Help your children understand the positive impact of giving. Discuss how even small acts of kindness can make a difference in someone's life. Talk about the various ways people can be helped through charitable organizations, such as providing food, education, healthcare, or support during difficult times.

3. **Involve them in decision-making**: Encourage your children to participate in the decision-making process when it comes to giving. Discuss different causes or organizations together and let them choose which ones they feel passionate about supporting. This involvement helps them develop a sense of ownership and connection to their charitable actions.

4. **Discuss gratitude**: Teach your children the importance of gratitude and appreciation for what they have. Help them recognize their privileges and understand that not everyone has the same opportunities. This awareness can motivate them to share their blessings and give back to those in need.

5. **Start small**: Begin with simple acts of giving that your children can easily understand and participate in. It could be donating toys, clothes, or books they no longer use to a local shelter or encouraging them to share their time and talents with others. These small gestures build a foundation for a lifelong spirit of giving.

6. **Share stories and experiences**: Share stories of individuals or communities who have been positively impacted by acts of kindness or charitable giving. These stories can inspire empathy and compassion in your

children and help them develop a broader perspective and a desire to help others.

7. **Volunteer together**: Look for volunteer opportunities that you can do together as a family. This could involve serving meals at a soup kitchen, participating in a community cleanup, or organizing a fundraising event. These shared experiences create lasting memories and reinforce the importance of giving back.

8. **Discuss the joy of giving**: Talk to your children about the emotional rewards that come from helping others. Explain how the act of giving can bring happiness, fulfillment, and a sense of purpose. Encourage them to reflect on their own feelings when they engage in acts of generosity.

Remember, the goal is to instill a sense of empathy, compassion, and a desire to make a positive impact in the lives of others. By sharing the idea of gifting and charitable behavior with your children, you are nurturing their character and teaching them the importance of being kind, generous, socially responsible individuals and all-round good citizens.

Notes:

....

....

....

Money Fact: There are over 1.4 million charitable organizations in the US.

Chapter 26.

What Resources are Available to Teach Personal Finance?

There are various educational resources you can use to teach your children about personal finance and money management. Here are some suggestions:

1. **Books**: There are numerous children's books like *M is for Money*, *Grandpa's Fortune Fables, Milton* and many more that are available that teach financial concepts in a fun and engaging way. Look for age-appropriate books that cover topics such as saving, budgeting, entrepreneurship, and the value of money. Check out www.cashcrunchgames.com for more resources.

2. **Online Videos and Websites**: Utilize online platforms that offer educational videos and interactive resources for kids. Websites like *CashCrunchGames*, *Khan Academy*, *PBS Kids*, *Sammy the Rabbit*, Bizkids, EasyPeasy Finance and *National Geographic Kids* often have sections dedicated to financial literacy and money management. A comprehensive list will be added in the resource section of the book.

3. **Board Games**: Board games like *Monopoly*, *The Game of Life*, *CashCrunch Junior* or *Money Bags* can provide hands-on learning experiences for children. These games simulate financial scenarios and decision-making, allowing kids to practice money management skills in a fun and interactive way.

4. **Mobile Apps**: There are several mobile apps designed specifically for teaching kids about money. Examples of the apps include: *Famzoo, Greenlight*, *GoHenry, Fidelity* and *BusyKid*. These apps provide virtual banking experiences, budgeting tools, and interactive games to help children learn about money.

5. **Workbooks and Activity Sheets**: Look for workbooks or activity sheets that are focused on financial literacy. These resources often include exercises, puzzles, and quizzes that reinforce key concepts and help children practice money management skills. See lists of resources on www.cashcrunchgames.com (will be updated periodically).

6. **Local Community Programs**: Check to see if your local community offers any financial literacy programs or workshops for kids. These programs might cover topics like budgeting, saving, and basic financial concepts. Enrolling your children in these programs can provide valuable

hands-on learning experiences and opportunities to interact with other children interested in financial education.

7. **Financial Literacy Websites**: Explore websites dedicated to financial literacy for kids and teenagers. Websites like *Practical Money Skills for Life, Money as You Grow, and City Pay it Forward* offer resources, games, and interactive tools to teach kids about money management.

8. **Personal Experiences and Conversations**: Share your own financial experiences and wisdom with your children. Engage in conversations about money, saving, spending, and budgeting. Use real-life examples to illustrate financial concepts and help them understand the practical aspects of money management.

There are so many resources for all ages from toddler to adult. It is just a case of going to your local library, stores (brick and mortar and online) and websites. Remember to select resources that are age-appropriate and align with your children's interests and learning styles. There are reading books, games, quizzes, videos, activities and so much more. Combining various educational resources will provide a well-rounded approach to teaching financial literacy and help your children develop a strong foundation in money management skills.

Notes:

....

....

....

....

....

....

....

....

....

....

....

....

....

....

....

....

....

Resources:

Visit **www.cashcrunchgames.com** for a comprehensive list of personal finance resources and blogs addressing these issues.

Notes:

....

....

....

The information shared draws upon the collective knowledge and experiences of individuals, including grandparents, parents, educators, and researchers. It's important to note that these responses are general in nature and may not apply to every specific situation or individual circumstance. If you're seeking more in-depth or specialized information, it's recommended to consult relevant books, research articles, educational resources, or seek advice from professionals in the respective fields.

Congratulations!

By reaching the conclusion of "Parents Raising Money-Smart Kids: A Guide for Ideas and Conversations", you've taken the first step towards equipping your children with the essential tools for financial success. Through the pages of this book, you've discovered the power of your role as a parent in shaping their financial destiny.

Now armed with practical strategies, insights, and a wealth of knowledge, you're ready to lead by example and impart invaluable lessons on money management. From setting a financial foundation to teaching smart spending choices, budgeting, and saving, you have the power to ignite a lifelong passion for financial responsibility within your children, plus it will save you a fortune in the long run and reduce the level of worry that you may have you that your child is not set up financially.

As you close this book, remember that you are not only a parent but a trusted money mentor and guide. Your dedication to raising money-smart kids will have a lasting impact, empowering them to navigate the complexities of the modern financial landscape with confidence, wisdom, and resilience.

Your commitment to raising money-smart kids will ripple through time, leaving a legacy that transcends generations.

The future is bright, and it's time to embark on this transformative journey together. Your children's financial success starts now!

About the Author

Paul Vasey is a former educator and financial literacy advocate. Although, now out of the classroom, he is still an educator at heart. He has taken what he has learned in the classroom, along with personal experiences and insights and has joined the battle to address financial illiteracy. He believes that money skills, habits and understanding should start at grass roots and that we all can learn from one another.

He also believes that storytelling and games create experiences and are great ways to start money conversations.

CASH CRUNCH GAMES